TELL ME ABOUT

ROALD DAHL

Acknowledgements

For permission to reproduce copyright material, the author and publishers gratefully acknowledge the following;

Cover Jan Baldwin **Title page** © Dahl Estate **page 5** Jan Baldwin **page 6 and 7** © Bremner & Orr Design Consultants Ltd 1996 **page 8** (left) Jan Baldwin (right) Sanjiro Minamikawa/Martyn F. Chillmaid **page 9** © Dahl Estate **page 10** © Dahl Estate/Martyn F. Chillmaid **page 11** © Dahl Estate **page 12** © Dahl Estate/Martyn F. Chillmaid **page 13** (top) © Dahl Estate/Martyn F. Chillmaid (bottom) Jan Baldwin **page 14** © Dahl Estate **page 15** (left) © Dahl Estate/Martyn F. Chillmaid **page 16** (top) Jan Baldwin/Martyn F. Chillmaid (bottom) © Dahl Estate **page 17** Jan Baldwin **page 19** © Dahl Estate/Martyn F. Chillmaid **page 20** Leonard McComb/Martyn F. Chillmaid © Life Magazine
Back cover © Dahl Estate

For more information about the Roald Dahl Museum and Dahl Foundation, you can write to the following address:

92 High Street
Great Missenden
Buckinghamshire HP16 0AN

TELL ME ABOUT WRITERS

ROALD DAHL

written by
Chris Powling

Evans

Evans Brothers Limited

VISIT OUR WEBSITE
www.evansbooks.co.uk

Published by Evans Brothers Limited
2A Portman Mansions
Chiltern Street
London W1U 6NR

© Evans Brothers Limited 1997

First published 1997
Reprinted 1998, 1999, 2000, 2001, 2002, 2004
First published in paperback by
Evans Brothers Limited in 2004

Printed in China by WKT Company Ltd

British Library Cataloguing in Publication data.

Powling, Chris
  Roald Dahl. - (Tell me about writers)
  1.Dahl, Roald, 1916-90 - Biography -Juvenile literature
  2.Authors, English - 20th century - Biography - Juvenile
  literature
  I.Title
823.9'14

ISBN 0237526212

Have you heard of Fantastic Mr Fox? Or read about The Enormous Crocodile? Do you know what was so scary about The Magic Finger? If you say yes to these questions then you are probably a fan of Roald Dahl already. If you say no, don't worry... it means you are in for a treat! For Roald Dahl was one of the most successful writers for children who ever lived. This is his story.

Roald Dahl in his famous writing hut

When Roald Dahl died, in November 1990, the eighteen books of stories and rhymes he wrote for young people had sold millions of copies all over the world. Today, he is just as popular as when he was alive. There is even a special Roald Dahl Museum you can visit, and concerts where you can hear his words set to music.

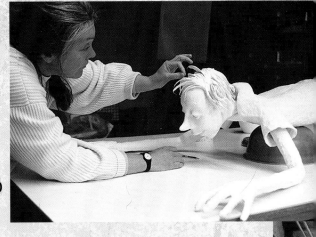

Making a model (above) and having fun (left and right) at the Roald Dahl Museum in Aylesbury in Buckinghamshire.

You can see his stories at the cinema, or on video in films like "Willy Wonka and the Chocolate Factory", or "James and the Giant Peach", or "Matilda".

Yes, Roald Dahl was a scrummdiddlyumptious storyteller!

His own life was almost as strange and exciting as some of the tales he told. He wrote about it himself in "Boy" and "Going Solo". It is clear from these books that he was always a bit of an outsider - someone who never quite behaved in the way people expected.

Roald the orchid-grower (above). A notice on his board (left) says he won first prize for one of his orchids.

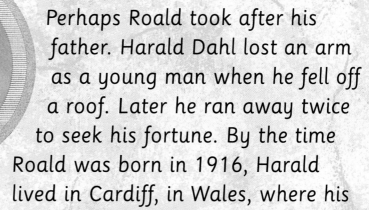

Roald's father, Harald

Perhaps Roald took after his father. Harald Dahl lost an arm as a young man when he fell off a roof. Later he ran away twice to seek his fortune. By the time Roald was born in 1916, Harald lived in Cardiff, in Wales, where his shipping business had made him rich. He died in 1920, so it was Roald's Norwegian mother who brought him up. They lived in a house called Cumberland Lodge, which Roald really loved.

Roald and his mother

Roald was less happy at boarding school. As soon as he could, he left for Africa to seek his own fortune.
There he spent two exciting years working for the Shell Oil Company.

Some of Roald's own photographs taken at Repton School.

Roald in Africa

In September 1939, though, Britain's war with Germany began and Roald decided to join the Royal Air Force in Nairobi as a pilot. Being a pilot was exciting, too … but also very dangerous. Roald had a bad crash in the desert - and his injuries made him limp for the rest of his life.

A painting of Roald by the artist Matthew Smith. Roald was a great collector of modern art.

After this Roald was sent to America as a kind of spy. While he was there he wrote a story about his adventures as a pilot. It was so good it was published in a famous magazine. Soon Roald was writing other stories - including one called "The Gremlins". Walt Disney loved it. He invited Roald to Hollywood so it could be made into a film.

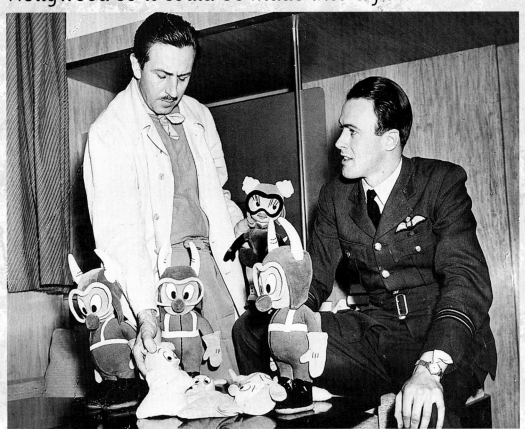

Roald with Walt Disney and the Gremlins

The film was never finished, but Roald's career as a writer had begun. After the war he lived partly in England and partly in America. He married an American film star called Patricia Neal. They bought a small farmhouse, called Gipsy House, in Buckinghamshire in England. They had five children - Olivia, Tessa, Theo, Ophelia and Lucy.

Roald and Patricia

Gipsy House

Between 1960 and 1965, three terrible things happened. The first disaster was Theo's. When he was a baby, his pram was hit by a taxi in New York. His brain was badly damaged. Straightaway, Roald started work with a doctor and an aeroplane modeller. Together they invented a gadget, called the Wade-Dahl-Till valve, to help children who had been hurt like Theo. Luckily, Theo got better by himself, but the valve saved the lives of thousands of other children.

Theo Dahl, who now lives in America

Later, something worse happened. If you read "The BFG" you will see it has a special dedication, to Roald's daughter Olivia. She died from a very rare kind of measles.

Even then the Dahl family troubles were not over. Roald's wife Patricia had a serious illness called a stroke. To help her recover, Roald organised a team of friends and neighbours to talk and play games with her every day for month after month. Two years later she was able to start filming again.

ROALD DAHL

The BFG
Illustrated by
QUENTIN B...

For Olivia
20 April 1955–17 November 1962

Patricia with Olivia and Tessa

Amazingly, while all this was going on, Roald was becoming more and more successful as a children's author. His first stories were based on bed-time tales he told his own children. He did his writing in a plain, cobwebby shed tucked away behind the orchard at Gipsy House.

Roald's writing hut(right) and a picture he took of Dylan Thomas's writing hut. Roald loved Thomas's poetry.

First he would settle down in an old, battered armchair with a wooden board propped across it. Then he would sharpen six yellow pencils. Gradually, hour by hour, he would wear these out writing on a pad of yellow paper. 'One of the nice things about being a writer,' he once said, 'is that all you need is what you've got in your head and a pencil and a bit of paper.'

Inside Roald's hut

ROALD DAHL

George's Marvellous Medicine

Illustrated by
QUENTIN BLAKE

What Roald Dahl had in his head was "The Twits", and "George's Marvellous Medicine" and "Esio Trot and The Minpins", as well as "The Giraffe and the Pelly and Me". Slowly, steadily, Roald Dahl's books made him one of the richest and most famous writers for children there has ever been.

Of course, that does not mean life was always easy. Plenty of grown-ups did not like his writing at all - and still don't. 'He's too rude,' they complain. 'He only appeals to the bad side of children. His stories won't make them better people.'

You must make up your own mind about that.

ROALD DAHL

The Giraffe and the Pelly and Me

Illustrated by Quentin Blake

A model of the BFG for the Dahl Museum

In 1983 Roald Dahl won a big prize for "The BFG". This book has pictures by Quentin Blake, who based the drawings for The Big Friendly Giant on Roald Dahl himself.

Quentin Blake and Roald Dahl at work at Gipsy House

Roald Dahl with his son Theo and young friends

After Roald's death, his second wife, Felicity Dahl, set up the Roald Dahl Foundation. This charity helps children and adults with serious illness and with problems with reading and writing. Roald Dahl would have loved this. He once said, 'I suppose I could knock at the door of any house where there was a child - whether it was in the US, Britain, Holland, Germany, France - and say "My car's run out of petrol. Could you please give me a cup of tea?" And they would know me. That does make me feel good!'

To feel good yourself, why not read one of his stories?

Important dates

1916   Roald Dahl was born

1925   He begins at St Peter's Prep School Weston-super-Mare

1930   He goes to Repton School

1938   Roald arrives in Africa

1939   He joins the RAF

1941   His injuries stop him flying

1942   Roald's first story "A Piece of Cake" is published in America

1942-61   He writes short stories for adults

1953   He marries the film star Patricia Neal; he moves to Gipsy House

1961   He publishes "James and the Giant Peach", his first children's book

1964   "Charlie and the Chocolate Factory" is published

1967   He scripts the James Bond movie "You Only Live Twice"

1983   He wins the Children's Book Award for "The BFG"; he wins the Whitbread Award for "The Witches"; he divorces Patricia Neal and marries Felicity d'Abreu

1989   He wins the Children's Book Award for "Matilda"

1990   Roald Dahl dies

Keywords

boarding school
a school where the pupils live during term-time

foundation
a charity which raises, and spends, money for good causes

gallery
a place where pictures, or interesting objects, are on show

magazine
like a book, often with pictures, which is published regularly

Index